THIS BOOK BELONGS TO

_____

For my family and friends.

This book is dedicated to you, young reader.
With sadness for what should not have been lost
and hope for what can still be protected.

J.M.

This book would have been lost without Dr Hazel Richards, Caroline Foster and Alice Sutherland-Hawes for their time and expert knowledge.

LOST

JESS McGEACHIN

WELBECK
EDITIONS

Published in 2024 by Welbeck Editions
An Imprint of Hachette Children's Group,
Carmelite House, 50 Victoria Embankment, London EC4Y 0DZ

Text and illustrations © Jess McGeachin 2024

Jess McGeachin has asserted his moral right to be identified as the author and Illustrator of this Work in accordance with the Copyright Designs and Patents Act 1988.

All rights reserved. No part of this publication may be reproduced, stored in a retrieval system, or transmitted in any form or by any means, electronically, mechanical, photocopying, recording or otherwise, without the prior permission of the copyright owners and the publishers.

A CIP catalogue record for this book is available from the British Library

978-1-80338-054-4

Printed in Heshan, China

10 9 8 7 6 5 4 3 2 1

CONTENTS

6 **Lost in the moment**

8 **Lost worlds**
10 Tooth and claw
12 New beginnings
14 Meet the megafauna
16 Say hello to the sapiens

18 **Lost cities**
20 Remains to be seen
22 The shadow of Vesuvius
24 Sunken cities

26 **Lost at sea**
28 All that glitters
30 A journey of endurance
32 Follow the light

34 **Lost in the wild**
36 Hiding in plain sight
38 Clever costumes
40 Time for a change
42 The way back home

44 **Lost forever**
46 A legacy of loss
48 Under threat
50 Back from the brink
52 The rest is up to us

54 **Lost and found**
56 Into the wild
58 A second chance

60 **Lost worlds compass**
61 **Find your way**
62 **Glossary**
63 **Index**

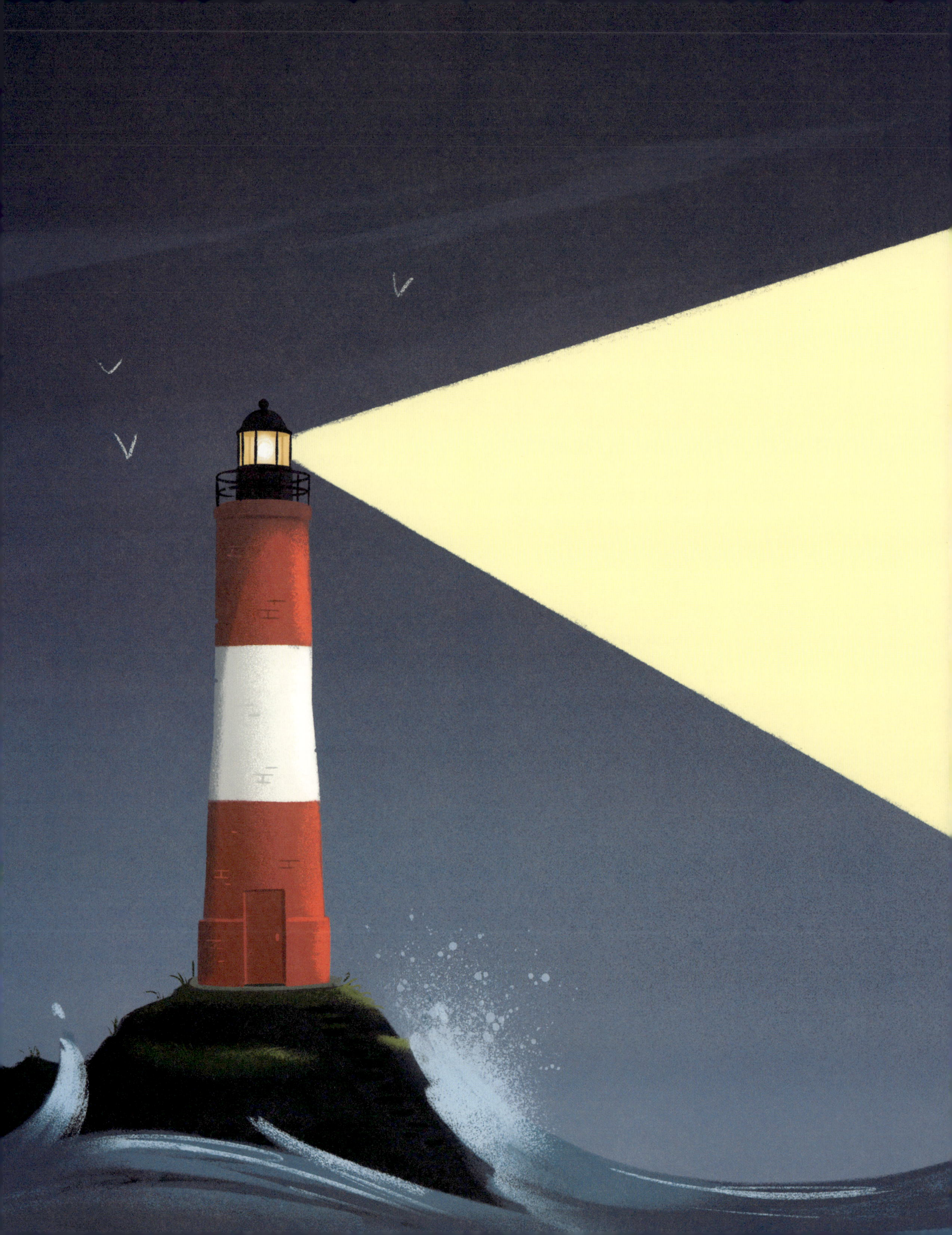

LOST IN THE MOMENT

We're about to embark on a journey through time to meet creatures and people who lived long ago.

Stroll the streets of ancient cities and set sail on a wooden ship into the unknown. No adventure is without its dangers, so watch out for sharp-toothed tigers, slippery sea monsters and those unexpected asteroids.

While there are lots of amazing things in the past, some of the most interesting creatures live on Earth right now. Colour-changing foxes, fashion-forward crabs and moths who wear eyes on their wings all call our world home.

It's a home that sometimes we forget we share, and sadly many species have already been lost forever.

It might be time for a different direction. Don't worry if you lose your way — we can always find a new path forward.

CALL OF THE CRETACEOUS

The deep past was a noisy place. *Parasaurolophus* grew hollow crests on the back of their heads which they might have used to make low, horn-like calls. Palaeontologists have even recreated the sound using digital models of their fossilised skulls – a lost song played for the first time in 67 million years.

SPOT THE DIFFERENCE

Have you noticed that some things here look pretty familiar, such as the sweet-smelling flowers in bloom or the dragonflies dancing on the breeze? By the time the Late Cretaceous Period rolled around, many of the plants and insects we know today had already started to appear.

LIFE IN COLOUR

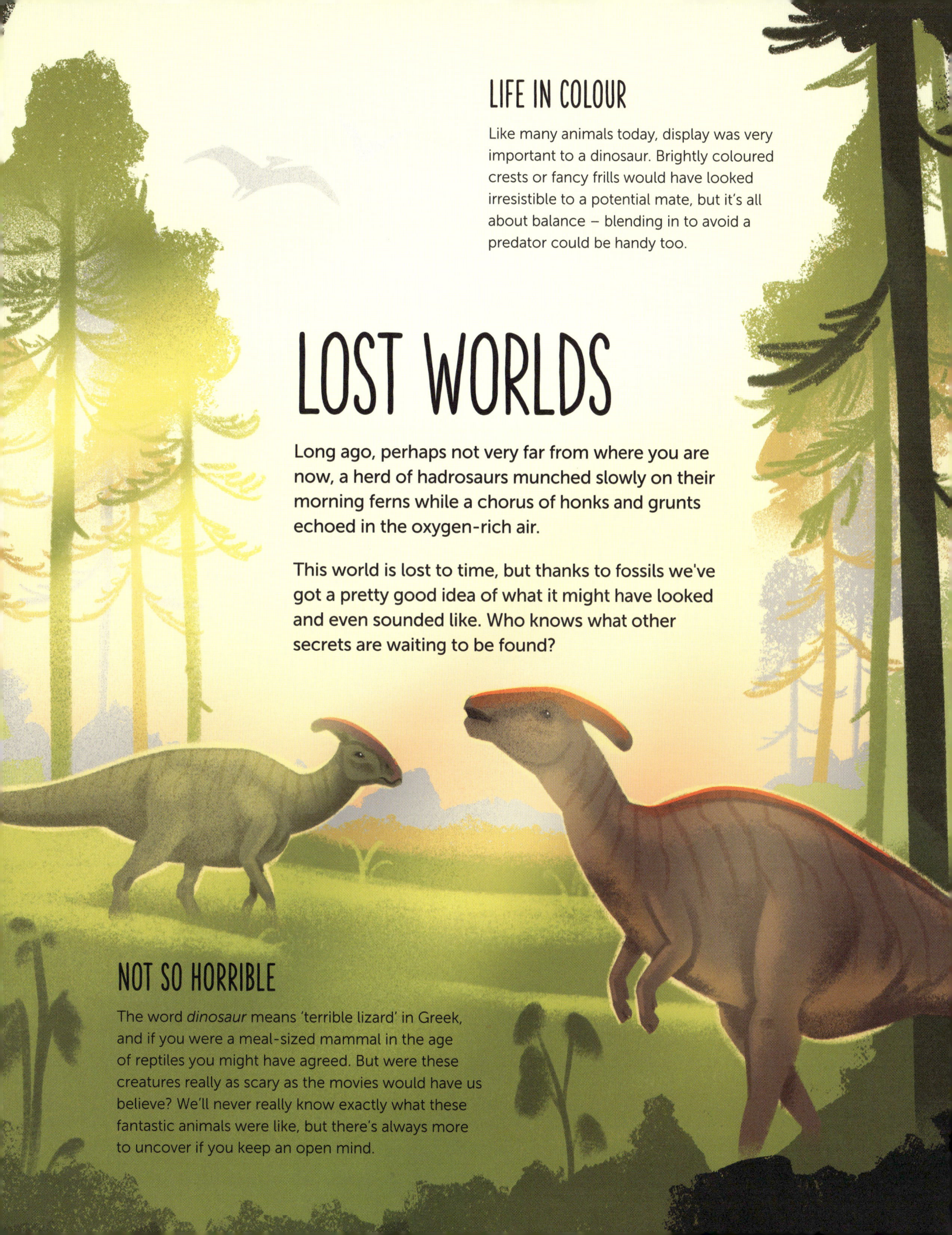

Like many animals today, display was very important to a dinosaur. Brightly coloured crests or fancy frills would have looked irresistible to a potential mate, but it's all about balance – blending in to avoid a predator could be handy too.

LOST WORLDS

Long ago, perhaps not very far from where you are now, a herd of hadrosaurs munched slowly on their morning ferns while a chorus of honks and grunts echoed in the oxygen-rich air.

This world is lost to time, but thanks to fossils we've got a pretty good idea of what it might have looked and even sounded like. Who knows what other secrets are waiting to be found?

NOT SO HORRIBLE

The word *dinosaur* means 'terrible lizard' in Greek, and if you were a meal-sized mammal in the age of reptiles you might have agreed. But were these creatures really as scary as the movies would have us believe? We'll never really know exactly what these fantastic animals were like, but there's always more to uncover if you keep an open mind.

TOOTH AND CLAW

As dinosaurs evolved into different shapes and sizes, they didn't hold back. Crested ornithischians, sweeping sauropods and cunning theropods were all part of this diverse reptile family.

Palaeontologists are discovering new fossils all the time – blueprints for what lost giants may have looked like millions of years ago.

Velociraptor
Late Cretaceous
75 million years ago

THINK LIKE A THEROPOD

Theropods were a bipedal group of dinosaurs, meaning they walked on two legs. You might know some famous theropods (looking at you, *T. rex*) but others had fluffy feathers and even small, wing-like arms. They couldn't fly yet, but some would eventually evolve into birds.

Spinosaurus
Late Cretaceous
99 million years ago

Diplodocus
Late Jurassic
150 million years ago

Brachiosaurus
Late Jurassic
150 million years ago

WHY THE LONG NECK?

Sauropods were the vegetarian vacuum cleaners of the dinosaur world. Long necks helped them reach the highest leaves and furthest ferns without having to move their body much – a clever energy saver for the biggest land animals that ever lived.

Edmontosaurus
Late Cretaceous
73 million years ago

ORNATE ORNITHISCHIANS

Nobody can outdress an ornithischian. These veggie-loving herbivores were a large group of dinosaurs that included *Triceratops*. Hungry carnivores were a constant threat so horns, plates, spikes and frills were all popular choices for defence (and to show off a bit of course).

Stegosaurus
Late Jurassic
155 million years ago

FRILL SEEKERS

We know *Triceratops'* frill was full of blood vessels, so it might have blushed bright colours to attract a mate. Like the plates on a *Stegosaurus*, it could even have been used to regulate heat – soaking up the midday sun or cooling off when things got too hot.

Triceratops
Late Cretaceous
68 million years ago

ALL GOOD THINGS...

Dinosaurs adapted perfectly to survive on Earth, and they did – for millions of years. The biggest threat to their existence didn't come from our world, it came from the depths of space. Suddenly all of the things that helped these reptiles thrive became a big problem.

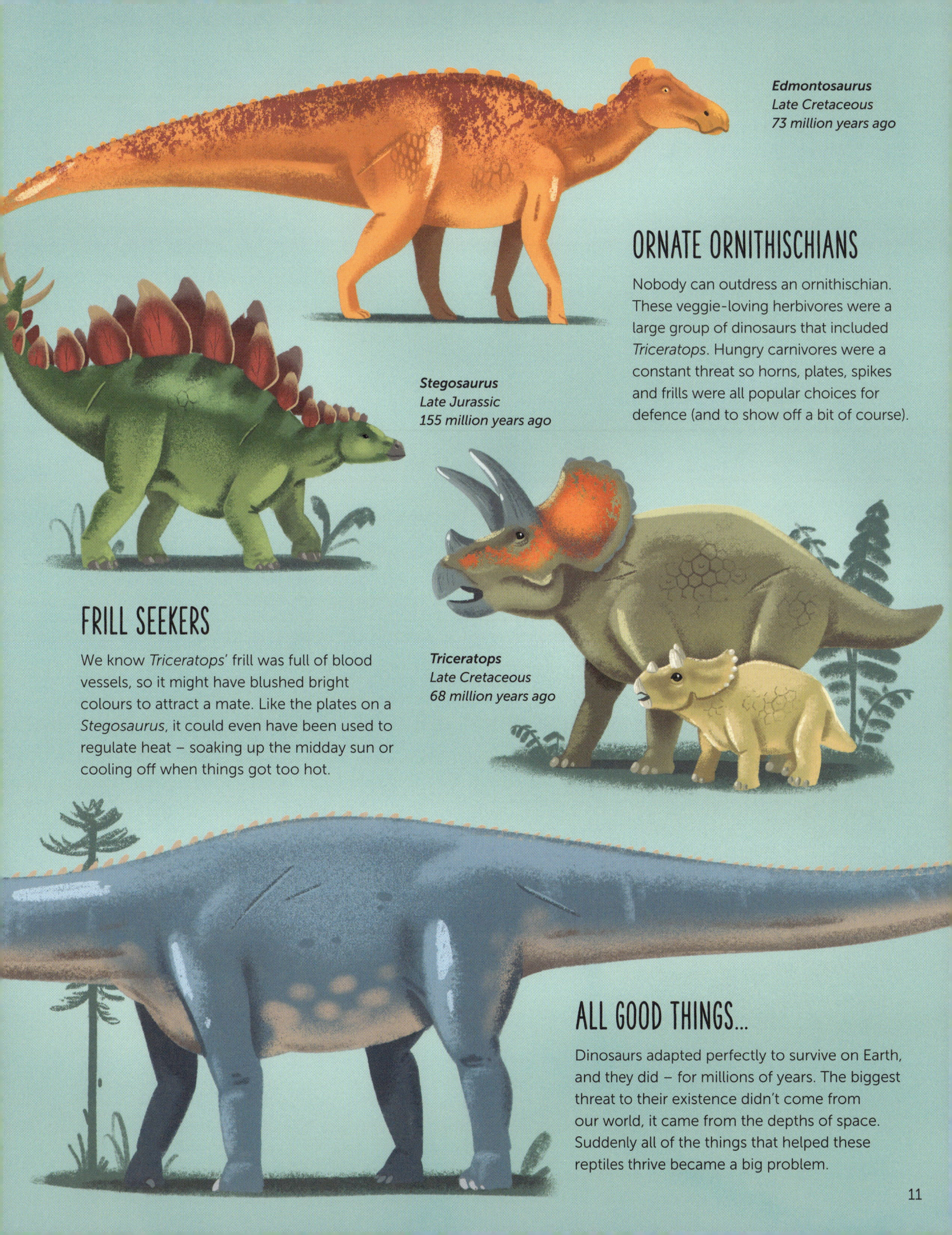

NEW BEGINNINGS

Every now and again a cataclysmic extinction event ruins a perfectly good day. When an asteroid slammed into the Yucatán Peninsula 66 million years ago, it eliminated three quarters of animal species on the planet including the last dinosaurs. That's the bad news, but the good news is that it opened up opportunities for new species to evolve – including us.

SMALL SURVIVORS

Sometimes hiding in your burrow is the safest place to be. Small mammals were able to scurry away and avoid the worst of the asteroid impact. Slowly they emerged, looking out at a whole new world. Their path ahead wasn't easy, but every mammal living on our planet today owes its existence to the few who stuck it out.

CROCODILES ROCK

If you've found the perfect design, why change? Crocodiles are cold-blooded creatures that are able to wait a long time between meals. Conserving all of that energy was a handy skill when food became scarce, and they've stayed pretty much the same ever since.

FEEL THE FERN

The world lost all of its forests in the extinction event that wiped out the dinosaurs, but from beneath the ash-covered ground tiny sprouts of green began to unfurl. Ferns and fungi grew back relatively quickly, spreading their spores far and wide on the wind.

WONDER CHICKENS

Scientists have found fossil evidence of a fowl-like bird that lived alongside the dinosaurs. Its small size and varied diet may have helped it survive the extinction event that wiped out nearly everything else. Respect the chickens.

MEET THE MEGAFAUNA

Without those dominant dinosaurs taking up all of the space, some of the mammals, birds and lizards left behind had an evolutionary growth spurt. They might have grown bigger to take advantage of the new types of food on offer or to better survive the colder temperatures. Most are now lost, but a few of their relatives survive – like the giant Komodo dragon.

Uintatherium
*Early Eocene,
50 million years ago*

Paraceratherium
*Early Oligocene
34 million years ago*

THINGS GET WEIRD

Some megafauna looked like jumbo versions of animals you can see today, but others are just wonderfully weird. *Paraceratherium*, a long-necked hornless rhinoceros, grazed on the grasslands of what is now Asia. It grew to nearly five metres tall and seven metres long!

Mammuthus,
*Late Pleistocene,
400,000 years ago*

ICE FOR SOME

Being big and hairy was an advantage in a cooler climate, one which mammoths used to spread far and wide (until things started to warm up again). We only just missed them – mammoths were still roaming northern Siberia while humans were building the pyramids in Ancient Egypt.

DON'T SMILE AT A SMILODON

The *Smilodon*, or sabre-toothed cat, is only distantly related to the big cats we know today. This muscular predator silently stalked through woodlands, ready to pounce on unsuspecting prey. Their curved teeth were up to 20 centimetres long – about the size of your forearm!

Smilodon
Early Pleistocene
2.5 million years ago

Glyptodon
Early Pleistocene
2.5 million years ago

Giant Moa
Mid Pleistocene,
1 million years ago

Palorchestes
Pleistocene
2 million years ago

MEANWHILE DOWN UNDER

Things in the Southern Hemisphere were starting to get bigger too. Giant marsupials like *Palorchestes* used their huge claws to shred vegetation while the venomous land lizard *Megalania* looked for other megafauna to snack on. Gulp!

Megalania
Pleistocene
1.5 million years ago

SAY HELLO TO THE SAPIENS

Look out of your window — what can you see? Is it a row of leafy treetops or the shoebox shapes of a city skyline? Twenty thousand years ago a group of prehistoric humans peered out from the mouth of a cave at a very different view, one crowded with roaming mammoths, bison and woolly rhinoceros. Luckily they didn't just look, they drew — lines sketched on rock that reveal a lost world.

PART OF THE FAMILY

We're just the latest in a long line of humans, with each species adding something special along the way. *Homo*, meaning human, is the title given to different branches of our family tree that include *Homo neandertalensi* and *Homo sapiens* (that's us!). We're the only species left, but that doesn't mean we'll be the last — who might come next?

DRAWN FROM LIFE

Late Ice Age peoples watched herds of the animals and carefully etched them on the walls of the *Grotte de Rouffignac* — The Cave of the Hundred Mammoths — in what is now France. Paintings like these are especially significant because they can tell us things about extinct animals that fossils can't — like the patterns on their fur.

FUTURE FOOTPRINTS

The humans who came long before us didn't leave much behind — ochre drawings and brittle bones that will soon fade to dust. We will leave lots of things in our wake, buried deep in the soft earth. Who will find them, and what stories will they tell?

STICKS AND STONES

Sharpening sticks and stone might have been one of the best ideas we've ever had (or borrowed from the chimps). Tools have let us light fires, build shelter and hurl spears at each other. They've also allowed us to change the landscape in which we live – for better or worse.

SHOW AND TELL

Lost cities make great stories, which is why you're reading about them right now. Sites like Machu Picchu are incredibly important for tourism, and can bring income to those who need it most. Too many heavy feet can trample on what was already once lost, so remember to tread lightly as you go.

LIKE BLOCKWORK

Great cities like Machu Picchu were built by slaves and workers whose names were forgotten, yet their skill is the reason the city is still standing. Each granite block fits perfectly together without mortar, so when an earthquake rumbles, the stones simply dance and fall back into place.

HIDDEN IN THE CLOUDS

The Spanish conquistadors had a habit of invading everywhere they went. The Inca Empire, like its Aztec neighbour, fell in the 16th century. The colonisers were intent on taking as much as they could, but they never found the city hidden in the mountains. Perhaps this is the only reason we can still see it today.

SACRED CITADEL

We don't know exactly what Machu Picchu was built for, nor why it was later abandoned. The Inca didn't write down their secrets, but archaeologists think it might have been a sacred spot to worship the gods, observe the heavens or for a king to show off their empire.

LOST CITIES

Perched in the mountains of Peru stands the Inca citadel of Machu Picchu. Stone temples cling to the cliffs while swirling fog fills the valleys below. A city once lost for 400 years.

But what does it mean to lose a city? Is it when the last villager leaves their home, forced out by climate or conflict? Or when its walls slip into ruin, forgotten by all those who came after?

REMAINS TO BE SEEN

Finding a lost city is a little bit like looking for a giant dinosaur fossil. You might only see the tip of its skull poking out from the sand, but dig a little deeper and the bones of buildings and the spine of city walls are revealed. Some of the earliest civilisations on Earth are still waiting under the desert — and we've only just found their noses.

Persepolis
(Present day Iran)
515 BCE

Ziggurat of Ur
(Present day Iraq)
2100 BCE

Arch of Ctesiphon
(Present day Iraq)
400 BCE

CITIES IN THE SAND

Today the world's oldest cities aren't much more than rock and rubble, but they were once rich, fertile places. The Mesopotamian city of Ur once dipped its toes in the Euphrates River and at its heart stood the great ziggurat temple. Slowly the river shifted and the city fell — drought, not armies, caused its decline.

Petra
(Present day Jordan)
400 BCE

CARVED IN STONE

Sometimes it's easier to build into the landscape rather than on top of it. The Nabataeans carved the city of Petra into the rosy-red sandstone cliffs that surround it. They built monasteries, tombs and complex water channels into the rock to create a hidden oasis in the middle of the desert.

Sigiriya
(Present day Sri Lanka)
5th century CE

FIT FOR A KING

If you're building a stronghold to stay safe from your enemies, the harder it is to get to, the better. Sigiriya is a rock fortress that rises from the forests of central Sri Lanka. A palace in the shape of a lion once sat on its summit. Its ruins still remain, but the king it was built to protect was overthrown long ago.

Tikal
(Present day Guatemala)
3rd–10th century CE

Angkor Wat
(Present day Cambodia)
12th century CE

TANGLED TEMPLES

Often the most impressive buildings weren't built for the living. The Maya peoples built stepped pyramids at Tikal and the Khmer Empire built temples at Angkor to honour their Hindu and Buddhist faiths – those ancient walls are now overgrown with twisted silk cotton trees.

THE SHADOW OF VESUVIUS

Some cities are lost over centuries, slowly engulfed by the sands that surround them. Others are lost in a day, through sudden tragedy or conflict.

Pompeii was much like any other Roman city, except it lay in the shadow of Mount Vesuvius — an active volcano. The occasional rumble didn't worry the locals too much, until one autumn day in 79 CE, smoke began to billow from the mountain...

WHISPERS OF A LOST CITY

Pompeii, like many lost things, was rediscovered by accident. The construction of an underground waterway revealed decorated city walls buried for 1,500 years. At first the ruins were forgotten, then looted, and now form one of the most important archaeological sites in the world.

WHAT'S LEFT BEHIND

Carbonised loaves of freshly baked bread, a perfectly preserved chariot and countless pots and coins have all been found at Pompeii, showing us what everyday life was like here nearly 2,000 years ago. Sadly ash from the eruption also preserved the shapes of people, forever in their final moments.

A DAY IN POMPEII

The seaside city of Pompeii was a vibrant, busy place. To visit the forum (a Roman town square) you would have first passed street stalls selling fresh fish, priests on their way to please the gods and sweaty townsfolk ready to relax and dive into the day's gossip at the public baths.

SCRATCHED IN STONE

Pompeii's painted walls show a colourful, creative city but to really get to know its people, look for the graffiti. There are names left behind ('*Gaius was here*'), petty insults ('*Oh, Epaphras, thou art bald*') and even early restaurant reviews ('*The food here is poison*'). Harsh.

SUNKEN CITIES

In the murky depths of the Mediterranean sea, a fallen pharaoh sleeps. He guards the ancient city of Thonis-Heracleion, an Egyptian trading port that sank into the sea nearly 2,000 years ago.

We tend to think about archaeology as digging through dirt in the desert, but most of our planet is covered in water — surely its best-kept secrets must lie under the sea.

SECRETS UNDER THE SURFACE

To find Thonis-Heracleion, archaeologists sent sonar waves across the sea floor and measured Earth's magnetic field to see if anything looked interesting under the waves. When it did, they used giant underwater vacuum cleaners to suck up the silt and reveal the lost city.

FACT OR FABLE?

Sometimes the line between history and myth can get a bit blurry. Atlantis was said to be a great golden city rising from the waves, until its people fell out of favour with the gods and the island was swallowed by the sea. Many people would say it's just a good story, but then again, most good stories start with a grain of truth.

TWO FOR ONE

For centuries, stories of two ancient lost cities were told – the Greek city of Heracleion, and the Egyptian port of Thonis. It wasn't until a team of divers found and translated a great *stele* (a stone carved with hieroglyphics) that they could confirm both cities were in fact the same one, Thonis-Heracleion – a city shared by both ancient Greeks and Egyptians alike.

FUTURE LOST CITIES

Losing a city might seem like a thing of the past, but rising sea levels mean that modern-day cities are at risk of disappearing too. Some countries are planning to move their sinking capitals, but it's at a cost not everyone can afford. What will future archaeologists find of these places? Will they even know where to look?

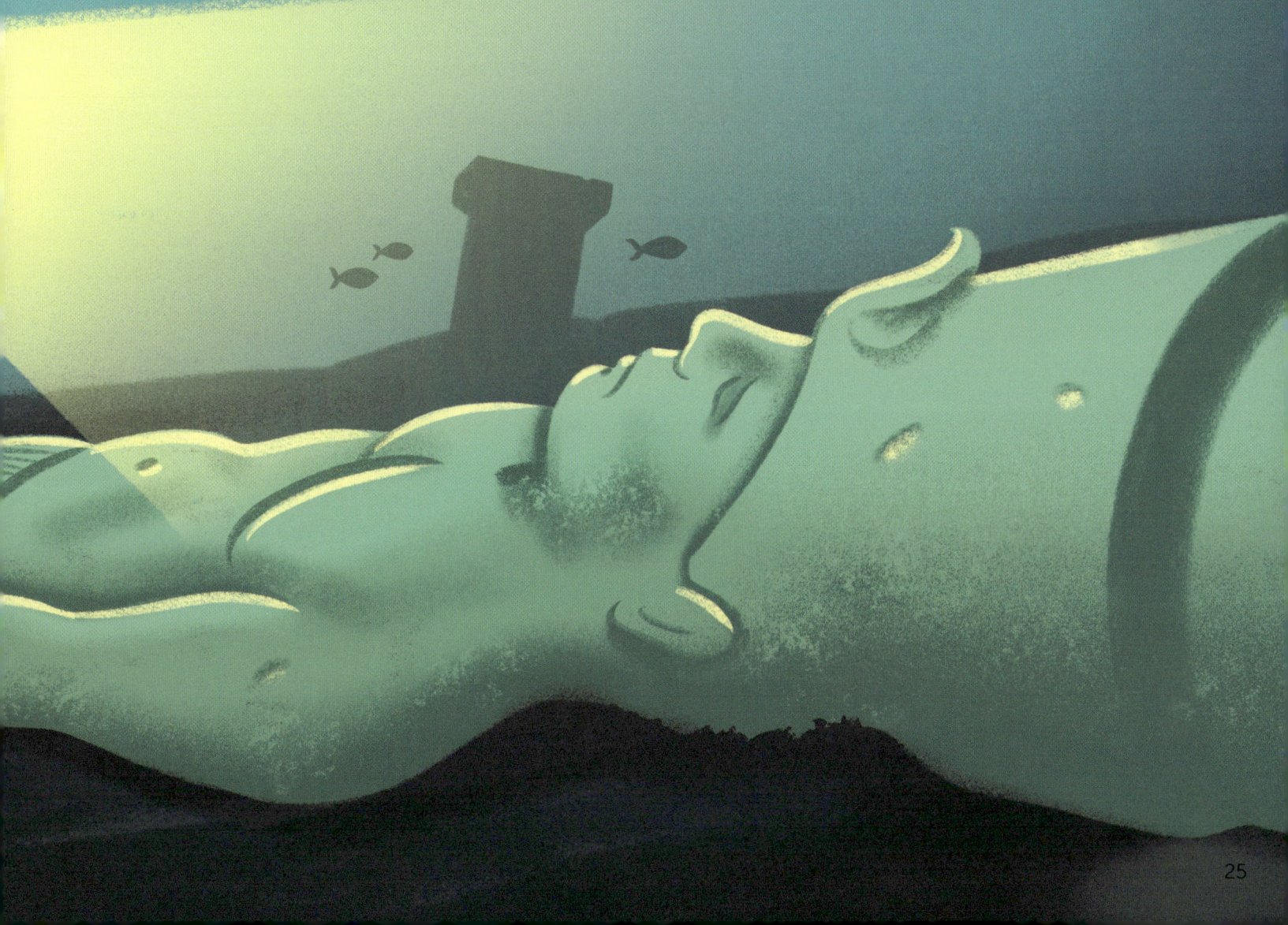

Galleon

INTO THE WAVES

For many ancient cultures, the azure horizon ahead offered much more than the dry land behind. Ancient Egyptians wove rafts from papyrus reeds, Phoenicians constructed wooden round ships and Polynesian navigators carved intricate two-hulled canoes. These different designs all shared the same goal – to sail across seas and safely back again.

HERE BE MONSTERS

Slippery serpents and fang-toothed monsters fill the parchment of medieval sea maps. Many sailors feared what they might find when they left the safety of land, so they drew them as a warning to others. Some were inspired by real-life animals, while others look much more mythical.

Phoenician ship

ONE PERSON'S JUNK...

It's all well and good to sail in a straight line, but if you want to turn easily you'll need a rudder. Ancient Chinese junks were the first ships to use rudders and sails reinforced by bamboo. They were easy to sail and were used to transport treasure and armies. They were even a popular choice for pirates!

Chinese junk

LOST AT SEA

People have crossed the ocean for centuries. They swapped goods, searched for new lands and undertook dangerous adventures just to prove they could.

The sea can be an unforgiving place, and you only need to look at the shipwrecks that lie on the sea floor to remember that not all of those voyages came home.

Dhow ship

Drua canoe

SAILING BY STARLIGHT

Polynesian sailors used the position of the Sun and the stars to navigate vast distances between islands, and looked for patterns in the wind, currents and even bird flight. Much of this knowledge was passed on through oral traditions like songs (a lot harder to get wet than a clumsy map).

THOSE WHO CAME BEFORE

While building ships and navigating the seas meant that some cultures could grow and thrive, it's important to remember that the land they 'found' often already belonged to others. Ships allowed empires to invade and steal lands that were, and still are, somebody else's.

ALL THAT GLITTERS

When some people think of shipwreck treasure, they imagine wooden chests overflowing with gold doubloons. In fact, hoards of these have been found and many more lie lost to the waves. For others, the real loot isn't jewels or coins — it's the stories. Letters from lost lovers, the music from forgotten melodies or even ancient maps of the sky.

Gold doubloons from the San José
Sank 1708

Letters from the SS Gairsoppa
Sank 1941

LOST LETTERS

When salvagers found the wreck of the SS *Gairsoppa*, a ship sunk in World War II, they were hoping to uncover a shipload of silver bars. Instead they found a different type of treasure — lost letters, written but never sent from passengers who didn't come home. One letter was returned to the author's family, 77 years after its postmark.

SHADOW OF A GIANT

Once thought to be unsinkable, the remains of *Titanic* are slowly disappearing from the Atlantic Ocean sea floor. Among the items recovered from her wreck are a bowler hat, a barnacled clarinet and a pair of brass binoculars — everyday objects with extraordinary stories to tell.

Objects from the RMS Titanic
Sank 1912

ANCIENT TECHNOLOGY

The ancient Greeks invented lots of clever things, including maybe the first computer. Archaeologists think pieces of a bronze device recovered from a Roman shipwreck may have been used to map the Sun and stars across the sky over 2,000 years ago. Unfortunately, it didn't come with an instruction manual.

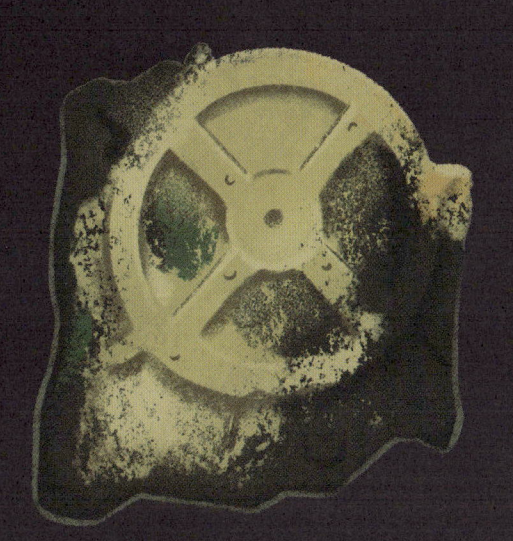

The Antikythera mechanism

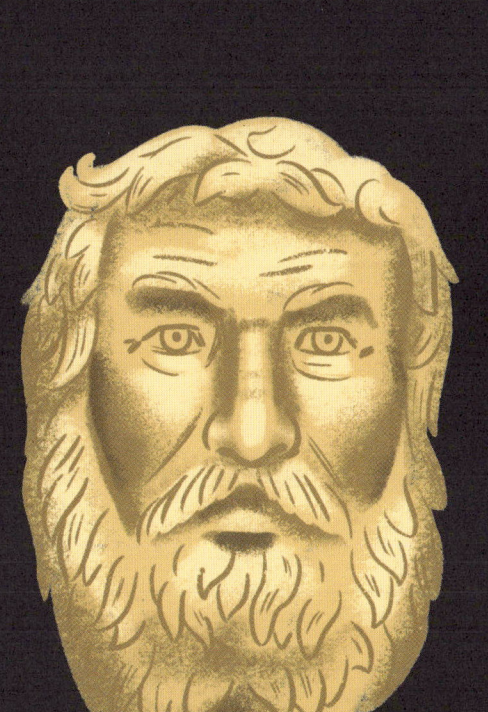

Objects fom the Caesarea wreck
Sank 400 CE

Ewer fom the Belitung wreck
Sank 830 CE

Philosopher statue from the Antikythera wreck
Sank 65 BCE

SALVAGED OR STOLEN?

Shipwreck artefacts can be worth a lot of money, but their real value can be easy to overlook. With so much culture resting in such fragile objects, we need to be careful in deciding who has the right to salvage them, or if they should even be removed at all.

A JOURNEY OF ENDURANCE

We humans like to try things that nobody else has done before, especially if it makes a good tale to tell our friends. For some, inventing a new type of sandwich will do (pineapple and peanut butter, anyone?) but for Ernest Shackleton it meant crossing Antarctica on foot for the very first time. Like all great expeditions, it didn't exactly go to plan… but somehow the best stories never do.

NO ONE LEFT BEHIND

The 28-strong crew of *Endurance* camped on the creaking ice for months before rowing to the remote Elephant island. From there, Shackleton and a small team embarked on a perilous journey for help. They returned four months later to rescue everyone left behind.

STUCK IN THE ICE

Shackleton and the crew of the *Endurance* set out from England in 1914, bound for Antarctica. They made it as far as the Weddell Sea, a maze of moving sea ice, before the ship became stuck and sank into the freezing water below. The crew were able to escape, but now they had another problem – they were stranded with no way home.

MOMENTS IN GLASS

Frank Hurley, the expedition's photographer, was able to capture the fated journey in photos and early moving images. Many of the moments captured had to be left behind, but a pocket full of film and a pile of plate glass negatives survived – a record of risk and courage at the edge of the world.

JOURNEY'S END

The *Endurance* remained lost under the ice for more than a century – until now. In 2022 a team of scientists combed the sea floor using remote submersibles and found an almost perfectly preserved shipwreck, the gilded letters ENDURANCE gleaming back at them from the darkness.

FOLLOW THE LIGHT

For the captain of a ship, the coastline can be a maze of jagged rocks and hidden reefs. A chart won't be of much use in the inky darkness, nor a compass for the stormy waves. Instead they might look for a lighthouse, its warm glow warning of hazardous waters ahead. Lighthouses have illuminated the way for seafarers since ancient times, and in many parts of the world they still do.

I'M STILL STANDING

Lighthouses have been built in all shapes and sizes. Four-sided fortresses, eight-sided oratories and round towers all rose above the ocean. Many lighthouses are adorned with fancy decorations. After all, if you're going to stand still for centuries, you might as well look good doing it.

THE SPARK OF AN IDEA

High above the ancient Egyptian city of Alexandria stood a tower of stone. The Pharos of Alexandria was the first (and tallest) ever lighthouse, a fiery beacon guiding ships into port. It survived kings and invaders but not the series of earthquakes which toppled it to the sea floor.

Pharos of Alexandria
Egypt, 280 BCE

Tower of Hercules
Spain, 1st century

St Catherine's Oratory
England, 1328

Lighthouse of Genoa
Italy, 1543

PRACTICE MAKES PERFECT

The Eddystone Lighthouse has been redesigned and rebuilt four times – the first from ornate timber (swept away in a great storm), the second from solid oak and iron (set ablaze from the spark of its lantern) and the third from carefully carved stone blocks. The fourth and current design builds on all of those which came before.

KEEPERS OF THE LIGHT

Lighthouse keepers are made of tough stuff. Grace Darling and her father, the keeper of the Longstone Lighthouse, rowed out in treacherous seas to rescue survivors from the Forfarshire wreck. Acts of bravery like these have ensured that lighthouse keepers fill the pages of history, even though there are far fewer of them working today.

Eddystone Lighthouse
England, 1759 (third design)

Cape Hatteras Lighthouse
North America, 1870

Peggys Cove Lighthouse
Canada, 1868

Les Eclaireurs Lighthouse
Argentina, 1918

NEW SEASON LOOKS

Arctic foxes wear a crisp, white coat in winter – but that wouldn't be much use in summer when the snow melts. Instead their fur changes from white to rocky brown. They're not the only ones: Arctic hares, lemmings and even snowy owls change their colour with the seasons too.

UNDER THE TUNDRA

The icy surface of the tundra is a dangerous place to be. Lemmings (a type of small rodent) build a network of tunnels to avoid a trip up above. Snow makes excellent insulation, and even Arctic bumblebees retreat underground in winter for a long, well-deserved sleep.

TRICK OF THE LIGHT

You know those bright-white polar bears? Look again – their skin is actually black and their hair mostly transparent! Tiny particles in the bear's fur scatter the light, illuminating their pelt in the morning sunshine.

LOST IN THE WILD

Survival is tough in the Arctic tundra. Howling winds chill the air and the frozen ground cracks under foot — there's enough to worry about without standing out in the barren landscape.

Luckily nature has plenty of hiding tricks: whether it's a colour-changing coat, light-reflecting fur or secret tunnels under the snow. Sometimes staying lost in the wild is the safest place to be.

PERMAFROST PROBLEMS

The tundra is changing, fast. It sits on the permafrost, a permanently frozen layer of ice and rock. As our climate warms, the permafrost is beginning to melt – releasing carbon and methane gases into the atmosphere, which in turn further warms the planet. Solutions require rapid action, but the animals of the Arctic remind us it's always possible to change your ways.

CLEVER COSTUMES

If you're looking for the best-kept fashion secrets, look no further than the natural world. Cunning creatures stay hidden by changing their skin, adding decoration or even putting on their own light show. If all of that doesn't work, they just copy someone else.

Beautiful wood-nymph

Stone grasshopper

PIGMENTS OF IMAGINATION

Crab spiders don't worry about webs to catch their prey. Instead they slowly change from white to yellow to match the flower they're sitting on. You'd think this was all about camouflage, but new studies suggest it might not help that much after all. Maybe they have trouble deciding what to wear too.

Crab spider

FAKE IT TILL YOU MAKE IT

The natural world is full of things pretending to be something else. Look closely at the forest floor and you might see a leaf-tailed gecko lost in the leaves. Moths have lots of tricks too – some wear wide-eyed spots while others look just like fresh bird poo.

Emperor moth

Eyelash leaf-tailed gecko

MASTERS OF DISGUISE

The ocean is the perfect place to see (or rather not see) clever camouflage. Creatures such as flounders, octopuses and cuttlefish have special cells called chromatophores. When squeezed, these tiny balloons fill with colour to create complex patterns that mimic their surroundings.

Octopus

Leafy seadragon

HAVE YOU REDECORATED?

Did you notice that clump of coral staring back at you? Decorator crabs dress up in disguise using objects they find. Algae, sponges and even plastic rubbish from the sea floor all make good materials. Leafy seadragons don't need to worry about dressing up – they already look just like seaweed.

Decorator crab

Pygmy seahorse

LIGHT UP THE DARK

A dark, squid-like shadow looks like a tempting snack to predators swimming below. Firefly squid use bioluminescence to match the brightness of the surface above. It's a trick called counter-illumination, nothing to see here, thank you very much!

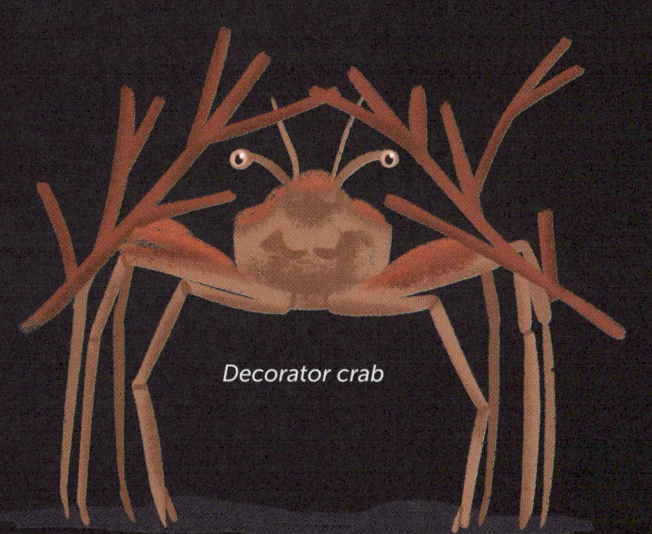

Firefly squid

37

HIDING IN PLAIN SIGHT

The golden grasslands of the African savannah are home to some of the most recognisable creatures on Earth – you just might not see them. Staying lost in this arid landscape is a matter of life and death, even if it's only by a whisker.

SPOT THE DIFFERENCE

Outlines are a bit of a giveaway in nature. Disruptive coloration is a way animals conceal their shape using patterns such as spots or stripes. It's much harder to see a cheetah against a patchy background if it's wearing patches too. Luckily the grazers know this as well. They're perfectly patterned to avoid being someone's dinner if they can help it.

Cheetah

Impala

African lion

SENSE OF NATURE

Every sense is an advantage in the natural world. Lions, who mainly hunt at night, have special mirrors in the back of their eyes to reflect moonlight and sharpen their sight. Like reptiles and amphibians, they have an extra organ in their mouths which they can use to 'taste' smells. Stinky impala? Delicious!

GOING ON STRIPE

We used to think a zebra's stripes were all about camouflage, but they might be helpful against a much smaller threat. Flies find it hard to land on a black and white runway, so the zebra avoids a nasty bite. The stripes could even help keep zebras cool, but we already knew they're the best-dressed guests at the party.

Giraffe

Zebra

39

TIME FOR A CHANGE

Things don't stay the same for very long in the natural world. Patterns change, colours shift and, if survival is at stake, you might need to change your look entirely. It can take a day, a lifetime or generations, but the next version might just be the best one yet.

Flamingo and flaminglet

PRETTY IN PINK

Flamingos start life as grey and fluffy, but a pigment called carotenoid in the algae they eat slowly turns them bright pink. Young harp seals have light-coloured fur to better absorb the sunlight and stay warm (before they gain some blubber) and green tree pythons begin life in banana-yellow before turning leafy green to hide in the treetops.

Adult and juvenile emperor angelfish

Harp seal and pup

Green tree python and snakelet

SENSING A PATTERN

Who said spots and stripes don't mix? Juvenile emperor angelfish swap their fingerprint-like rings for blue and yellow streaks as they grow up. Soft stripes help young wild boars (or boarlets) disappear in the undergrowth until they're big enough to protect themselves.

Wild boar and boarlets

THIS COULD TAKE A WHILE

When Charles Darwin visited the Galápagos Islands in 1835, he noticed something curious: the giant tortoises on different islands had their own, unique style. Some had domed shells and others had saddleback-shaped ones – allowing them to stretch out their necks and reach tall cacti. Had these species slowly changed to suit their environment?

WHERE TO NEXT?

Things haven't finished changing yet. When green anole lizards lost their home in the lower branches to an invasive species, they evolved bigger, stickier toes to move up higher in the trees. Tawny owls have started to change from snowy-grey to patchy brown to better blend into a warming world.

THE WAY BACK HOME

In some ways, finding your way in the world has never been easier. Many of us hold maps of the entire planet in our pocket, ready to be pinched and swiped at a moment's notice. In other ways, the right path to follow is often hard to find; the world can be a noisy place and it's changing all the time. Perhaps we can learn a thing or two from the smallest creatures – the ones who already know the way back home.

MAGNETIC ATTRACTION

It's easy to forget that we live on a giant, spinning magnet. Songbirds, salmon, sea turtles and many other animals use the Earth's magnetic field to navigate across vast distances. They can even find their way back to the exact breeding grounds where they were born, ready to mate and start the cycle anew.

MOVERS AND SHAKERS

When it comes to finding the perfect flower, honey bees have more than one trick up their abdomen. They can remember the landscape below, plot the position of the Sun and even smell their way back to the hive. But how do they share this information with other bees? They perform a special 'waggle dance', of course!

THE BEETLE AND THE STARS

For dung beetles, knowing which way to roll the poo they collect is essential. Scientists have shown that at least one species, *Scarabaeus satyrus* uses the light from the Milky Way to navigate. That same night sky is getting pretty crowded with satellites and bright lights – a reminder that our actions could cause even the smallest creatures to lose their way.

UNWELCOME GUESTS

The thylacine (or Tasmanian tiger) was a shy marsupial that once prowled the dry forests of mainland Australia – until it was forced to compete with a changing climate and the introduction of a new predator, the dingo. Thylacines disappeared everywhere except for the island of Tasmania, until a much more human threat emerged.

TWO WORLDS COLLIDE

Why do we label some creatures worthy of protection and others as pests? Rumour spread that thylacines were hunting farm animals, so the government offered a reward for every animal captured. The true culprit was much more likely to be feral dogs, but the damage was done – people are not kind to the things that they fear.

THE LAST OF A KIND

The last known thylacine spent her final days in a concrete cage at a zoo. It's not a very nice thing to think about, but it's important to remember the small space we left for an animal that once roamed a continent. The thylacine was granted protection just two months before they were gone forever.

LOST FOREVER

Extinction is nothing new on our tiny blue planet. Living things have come and gone, some staying for a short while and others for millions of years. But the rate at which we're losing plants and animals today *is* new. Species are disappearing faster now than at any point in modern history. Can we learn from our mistakes and slow the pace?

UNNATURAL SELECTION

Should we try to remake what we've lost? Scientists are close to unlocking the DNA secrets that could bring back extinct creatures like the thylacine and woolly mammoth. Would it be fair to reintroduce an animal to a world we've changed so much?

A LEGACY OF LOSS

The pages of our history books are filled with drawings and photographs of creatures we'll never meet. Some were lost through careless mistakes, but others were no accident – they were hunted for food and sport. We can't change the past, but we can make better choices to protect the species living right now.

WITHOUT A FLIGHT

Humans have not been kind to flightless birds. Animals like the dodo and the great auk were perfectly adapted to life on their small island homes, but they were easy targets for the sailors who landed there.

Dodo
Extinction: 1662

Great auk
Extinction: 1844

Bluebuck
Extinction: 1799

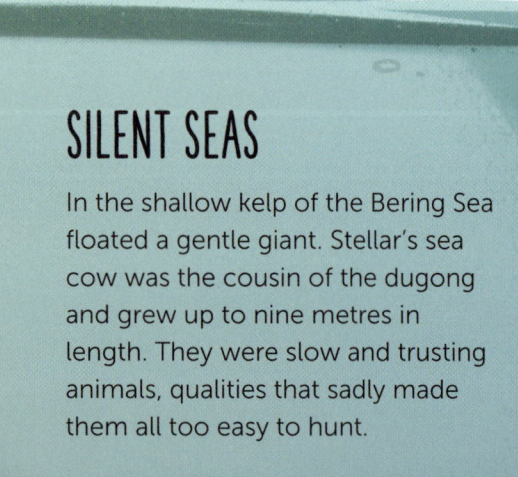

SILENT SEAS

In the shallow kelp of the Bering Sea floated a gentle giant. Stellar's sea cow was the cousin of the dugong and grew up to nine metres in length. They were slow and trusting animals, qualities that sadly made them all too easy to hunt.

Steller's sea cow
Extinction: 1768

Passenger pigeon
Extinction: 1914

FAILING THE SNAILS

Rosy wolfsnails were introduced in Hawaii to eat pests such as the African land snail. Except they ate nearly everything else too, including local, smaller snails like *Achatinella apexfulva*. The last member of this species died in captivity – his name was George.

Achatinella apexfulva
Extinction: 2019

ON OUR WATCH

There was a time when the skies over North America were filled with passenger pigeons. These huge flocks of bronze-bellied birds were the perfect target practice for the hunters below. A small prize for a much greater loss.

Xerces blue
Extinction: 1940s

Yunnan lake newt
Extinction: 1979

Golden toad
Extinction: 1989

Bramble cay melomys
Extinction: 2015

Smooth handfish
Extinction: 2020

WHAT WE DON'T KNOW

It's surprisingly tricky to call a species extinct. First you have to prove it *had* existed, and then you have to prove it hasn't been seen for decades. It's a lot easier to notice a big mammal disappear than it is a small fish. What else has been lost that we didn't even know was there in the first place?

UNDER THREAT

The International Union for Conservation of Nature (IUCN) keeps a list of living things that are under threat of extinction. It includes vulnerable, endangered, critically endangered and extinct species. It's a long list, and getting longer, but only by understanding the scale of the problem do we stand a chance of fixing it.

BENEATH THE SURFACE

The most impressive forests don't grow above sea level, they grow under it. Swaying kelp and colourful coral reefs are home to millions of sea creatures, many of which we've never even named. As our climate warms, our oceans are taking most of the heat – putting a third of all reef corals under threat.

GROWING PROBLEMS

Colourful birds and wide-eyed mammals might make the best calendar cover, but the plants and fungi that have grown up around us are also in decline. Two-thirds of all cycads, the same plants that fed the dinosaurs, are at risk of extinction. So too are a quarter of all flowering plants and a third of all trees.

ALL THE SMALL THINGS

Millions of insect species pollinate the food we eat, decompose the waste we leave behind and serve as a food source to the animals with whom we share our planet. Yet these tiny critters are in big trouble, and the chemicals we spray on our farms are a huge part of the problem.

THE RIPPLE EFFECT

Looking at a species in isolation can be helpful, but it doesn't always show the whole story. Every endangered flower means less pollen for an insect to harvest. Every bleached coral means one less hiding place for a fish. Luckily, positive actions can have ripples too, and each species protected and taken off the endangered list makes it easier for others to thrive.

BACK FROM THE BRINK

On the lush slopes of an extinct volcano, a family of great apes slowly chew their way through a lunch of stringy bamboo and wild celery. These are mountain gorillas, one of our closest animal relatives. They're a creature we came close to losing forever, but thankfully it looks like we might have acted just in time.

ONE OF THE FAMILY

Mountain gorillas live in large families, with everyone taking a turn to look after the young ones. They spend their days foraging, resting and rolling around in the sticky undergrowth, while the dominant silverback keeps a close eye on things. As the sun begins to set, they construct leafy nests for a well-earned snooze.

STUCK IN THE MIDDLE

Mountain gorillas have been caught up in some very human problems. Much of their forest home has been cleared for farming, and what's left bears the scars of conflict and poaching traps. They're also at risk from the same diseases that we are — gorillas share 98 per cent of our DNA.

THINK LOCAL

It's hard to think about protecting another species if you can't afford to feed your family. The communities near these last, wild places often don't have a lot of money and have made tough decisions to survive in the past. Tourism offers new opportunities to protect these amazing apes and for local people to make an income at the same time.

TURNING THE TIDE

Late last century, the number of mountain gorillas in the wild dwindled to less than three hundred. Through decades of campaigning and community support, they now number over a thousand. While they're still listed as endangered, it's a fragile success worth celebrating.

THE REST IS UP TO US

There was a time, not that long ago, when we nearly lost the largest creatures on our planet. Whales were hunted for their bones and blubber to make oil and outfits. In some places, they still are.

These gentle giants didn't disappear. We found a new path, and parts of the sea that fell silent are filling once more with song. If we can change our ways to protect the biggest things in our world, surely we can for the smallest, too.

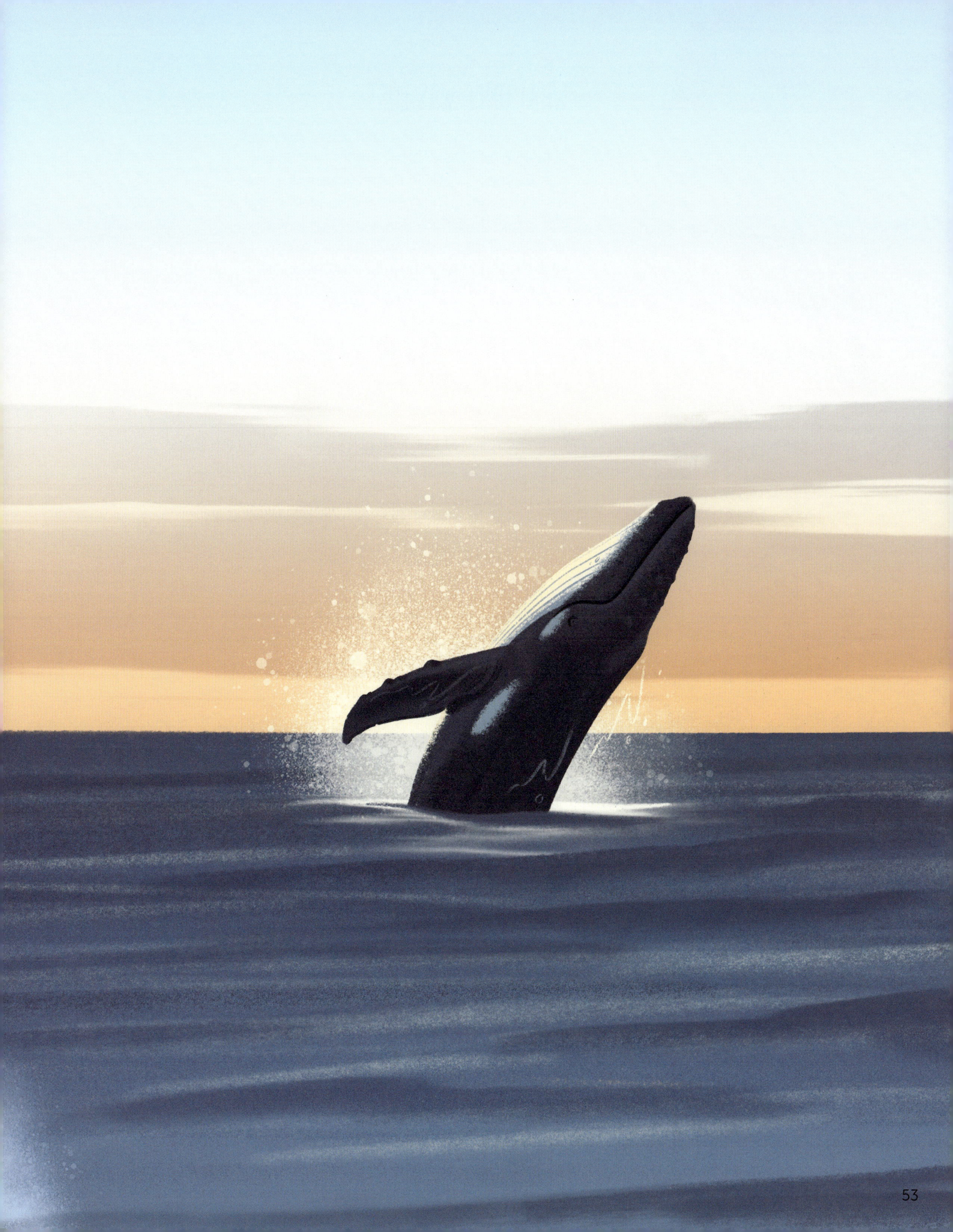

WHAT ONCE WAS LOST

Beavers were once widespread across the rivers of Europe, but when 16th-century gentlemen decided their fur would make excellent top hats and their scent glands perfect perfumes, they were driven to extinction in many countries. Now, hundreds of years later, they've been reintroduced into areas where they were lost.

THE BIG PICTURE

Beaver dams store carbon, slowing it from entering our atmosphere where it contributes to climate change. They can even reduce the impact of floods by reducing the flow of water downstream. There's lots of work ahead to fix these global problems, but we might have more help than we know.

ALL WORK (SOME PLAY)

Beavers are a keystone species, which means they do a lot of the heavy lifting to keep the ecosystem healthy. The dams they build slow rivers into ponds and create a wetland home for insects and frogs. The native trees they fell grow back bushier than before, making a perfect habitat for birds and other small animals.

LOST AND FOUND

Across the surface of a cool, Scottish river swims a family of busy builders, collecting sticks before the sun slips below the water. These are Eurasian beavers, the first to live there in four hundred years.

As humans, we've caused huge damage to the environment around us, but with careful planning and a bit of luck we might be able to slow the current — or maybe even change its course.

THE PLACES WE SHARE

A lot can change in four hundred years. Much of the woodland and winding rivers have become farmland, and some people worry the animals we reintroduce could compete with the industries we've built. It's a tricky balance, but we can find the path forward by talking together as a community. One stick at a time.

INTO THE WILD

The natural world is pretty good at finding the right balance. Grazing animals munch on grass and shrubs, leaving enough for the small birds to hide in. Large predators munch on the grazers, making sure there's not too many of them to eat all of the shrubs. And the small birds sit on the grazing animals, eating the tiny insects on their back in exchange for a free ride.

BACK TO THE SERENGETI

The number of blue wildebeest in the Serengeti of Africa rapidly declined due to disease in nearby cattle. Without the wildebeest, the grass grew thick and wildfires spread. Luckily, a vaccine was developed for the cattle and the blue wildebeest now migrate across the Serengeti in their millions once again.

Grey wolf

SOMETHING TO HOWL ABOUT

Grey wolves once roamed freely across Yellowstone National Park in the USA, but last century they were culled to extinction and the night sky fell silent. Without this apex predator, the growing population of elk overgrazed the land. Now that wolves have been reintroduced, much of the ecosystem is returning to balance.

Blue wildebeest

Galápagos tortoise

SLOW AND STEADY

Do you remember those Galápagos tortoises that were so important to our understanding of evolution? We let many of their species become endangered and even extinct. Through breeding programs, the numbers are now on the rise – thanks in part to a single tortoise who fathered a thousand kids!

WHERE'S WOYLIE?

Brush-tailed bettongs (or woylies) once hopped across two-thirds of mainland Australia, digging and replenishing the land as they went. These small, nocturnal marsupials were devastated by introduced predators, but now communities and First Nations leaders are helping the bettongs bounce back.

A SECOND CHANCE

High in the cloud forests of Ecuador, a team of scientists search the dense undergrowth for a ghost. They're looking for *Gasteranthus extinctus*, a bright orange flower named after its own extinction. Except it's not gone after all – a handful of its species cling on in the last fragment of the rainforest. Sometimes we do get a second chance to protect things we thought we'd lost forever.

A SECRET SANCTUARY

On a thin ridge below the Andes mountains grow plants that are found nowhere else in the world. More than 90 per cent of these damp forests were cleared to make way for farming, but by using satellite maps, scientists were able to spot slivers of green among the brown – the secret sanctuary of a lost flower.

NOT SO LOST

Sometimes we find a species that was once labelled as extinct. In the 1950s, a small colony of Bermuda petrels was spotted on a remote, rocky island in the North Atlantic Ocean – three hundred years after they were declared extinct. The seabirds, who only lay one egg a year, have slowly grown in number. They are still endangered but very much alive.

HOPE IN THE UNDERGROWTH

This isn't just a story about bright, beautiful flowers or soaring seabirds. These plants and animals are also incredibly important reminders thatt there's hope to be found when all seems lost – you just have to remember to look.

LOST WORLDS COMPASS

You didn't think we'd send you out to explore lost worlds without a map, did you? Use this compass to travel back in time and meet the people and creatures who lived there.

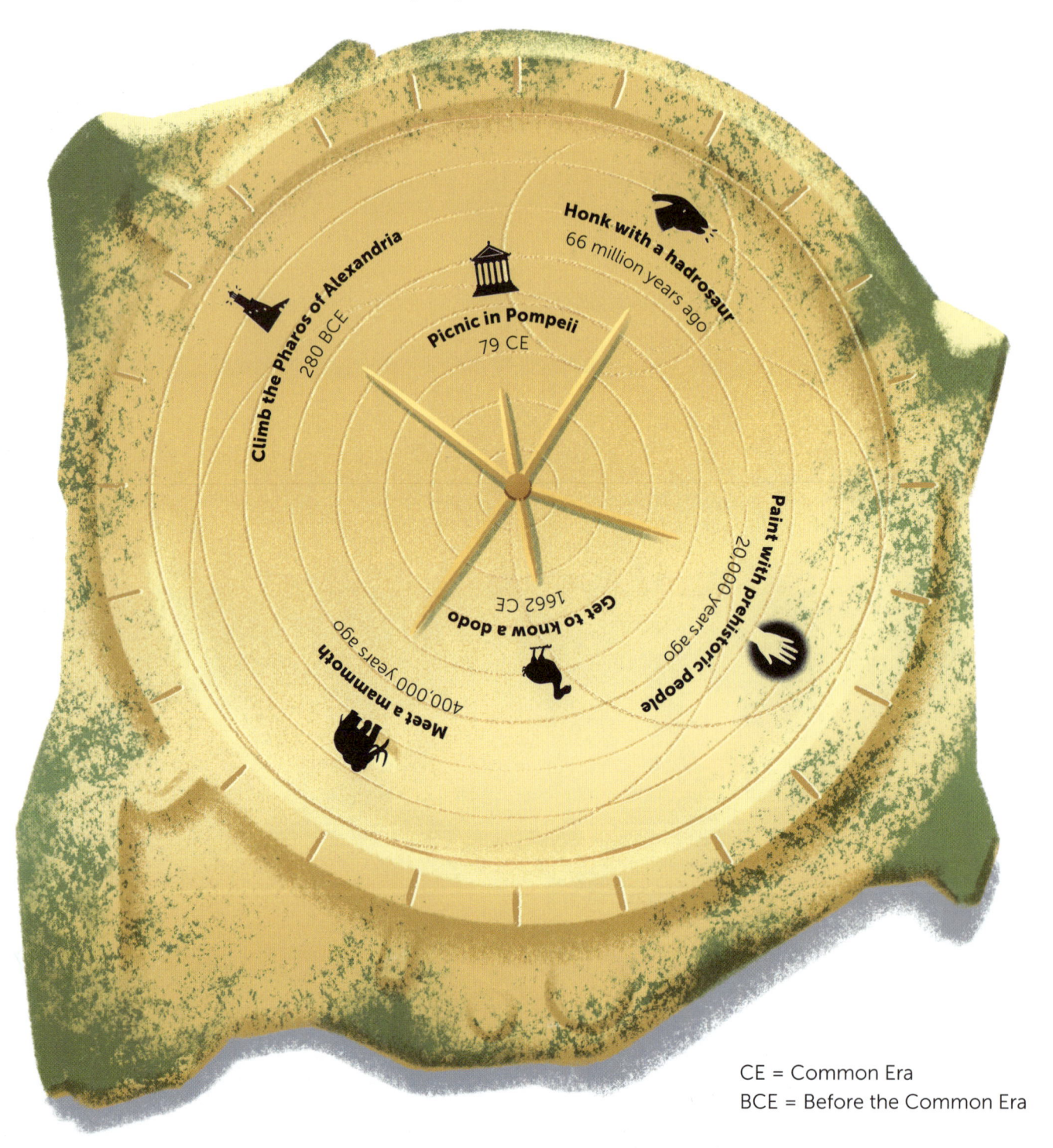

- Climb the Pharos of Alexandria — 280 BCE
- Picnic in Pompeii — 79 CE
- Honk with a hadrosaur — 66 million years ago
- Paint with prehistoric people — 20,000 years ago
- Get to know a dodo — 1662 CE
- Meet a mammoth — 400,000 years ago

CE = Common Era
BCE = Before the Common Era

FIND YOUR WAY

It can be tricky to navigate our wild, wonderful world.
Here are some directions from those who know the way.

MAKE SOME NOISE

If you're looking to find a new friend or warn off an enemy, make some noise. Roars, squawks or a long howl will do. If you leave some fossil clues behind, your sound might even echo through time.

DRESS TO IMPRESS

The natural world is full of fashionistas ready to strut their stuff. Fancy frills, colourful crests and a spiky tail are all good choices, or, if you'd rather blend in, try patterns and colour-changing skin (or just borrow someone else's look).

FOLLOW THE STARS

Dung beetles and seafarers share a secret — look for the brightest stars and you'll always find your way back home. Ancient astronomers even invented machines to track the Sun and moon across the sky... we just haven't found all the pieces yet.

LOOK BACK...

Humans have made some terrible mistakes. Entire species have been lost to greed and ignorance, and if we continue on our current path, many more will disappear. Look back at the actions of those who came before and decide what comes next.

...AND LOOK AHEAD

Our world still holds lots of secrets. If you think some of the creatures in this book are weird, imagine the fossils we've yet to find and the creatures living today that we've yet to meet. If we're really lucky, we might even rediscover things we thought we'd lost forever.

PASS IT ALONG

It's all well and good learning the secrets of the universe, but if you don't pass it along nobody else will know. Paint it on the wall of a cave, sing it in song or write it in a letter — just make sure to leave what you learn for someone else to find.

GLOSSARY

Archaeologist a scientist who studies the history of humans by looking at what man-made objects were left behind.

Bioluminescence the production and emission of light by a living thing. This is caused by a chemical reaction inside the bodies of certain creatures. An example would be a firefly, who can produce light from within its abdomen, or the firefly squid (see page 37) who uses the light it produces to camoflage itself from predators.

Disruptive coloration this is a form of camouflage where bold patterns are used to make it much harder to see the outline of animal.

Evolution this describes the way that living things change over time. Gradually, over millions of years, species adapt to the place they live, with each generation a little bit better or stronger than the previous one.

Extinction event this is when species of animals and plants vanish much faster than they are replaced. An extinction event occurs if around 75 per cent of the world's species is lost in a short period of geological time (less than 2.8 million years). An example of an extinction event was the asteroid strike that wiped out the dinosaurs.

Palaeontologist a scientist who specialises in studying life that existed in the far distant past.

Permafrost any area of ground or seabed that remains completely frozen for at least two years. The soil in a tundra is considered permafrost.

Tundra large areas of treeless plains in the far northern regions of the world. The bottom layer of soil in a tundra is permanently frozen and the low rainfall means that these areas are considered to be deserts.

INDEX

AB
amphibians 39
ancient Greeks 25, 29
animal display 8–9, 10–11, 61
  bioluminescence 37
  colour 40–41
archaeologists 19, 29
Arctic 34–35
beavers, Eurasian 54–55
bees, honey 43
birds 10, 14–15, 42, 46–47, 48, 55, 56, 58–59

C
camouflage 36–37, 38–39
cave paintings 16
cities 18–19, 20–21, 22–23, 24–25, 32
climate 14, 19
climate change 35, 44, 48, 54
conflict 19, 50
conservation 50–51, 52–53, 54–55, 56–57, 58–59
  returning to the wild 56–57
coral 37, 48–49
Cretaceous Period 8, 10–11
crocodiles 12

DE
Darwin, Charles 41
dinosaurs 8–9, 10–11, 12–13, 14, 20, 48
dung beetles 43
Egypt 14, 32
empires 19, 21, 27
  Inca 19
  Mayan 21
endangered 48–49, 51, 56, 58
Endurance 30–31
evolution 10, 12, 40–41
extinct animals 8–15, 44–48, 58
extinction 12–13, 45, 46–47, 48, 54, 56, 58
  event 12

F
flowers 8, 36, 43, 49, 58–59
forest 13, 21, 36, 44, 48, 50, 58
fossils 8, 9, 10, 13, 16, 20, 61
fungi 13, 48

GHIJ
Galapagos Islands 41
gods 19, 23, 24
grasslands 14, 38–39
humans 14, 16–17, 30, 46, 55, 61
insects 8, 49, 55, 56
International Union for Conservation of Nature (IUCN) 48
Jurassic Period 10–11

LMN
lighthouses 32–33
  Eddystone 33
  Alexandria, Pharos of 32, 60
Machu Picchu 18–19
mammals 9, 12, 14, 47, 48
mammoths 14, 16, 45, 60
mates 9, 11
mating 42
megafauna 14–15
mountain gorillas 50–51
navigation 26–27, 42–43

PQR
palaeontologists 8, 10
permafrost 35
Petra 20
planet 12, 24, 35, 42, 45, 49, 52
plants 8, 45, 48, 58–59
  ferns 9, 10, 13
Pompeii 22–23, 60
predators 9, 15, 37, 44, 56
reptiles 9, 10–11, 39
ruins 19, 21, 22

S
sabre-toothed cat 15
savannah 38–39
sea 24–27, 30, 33, 48, 52
  Bering Sea 46
  Weddell Sea 30
seafloor 27, 28, 31, 32, 37
ships 26–29, 30–31
shipwrecks 28–29, 31,
species 12–13, 16, 41, 43–49, 51, 54–59, 61

TU
Thonis-Heracleion 24–25
Titanic 28–29
tourism 18, 51
treasure 27, 28–29
Ur 20

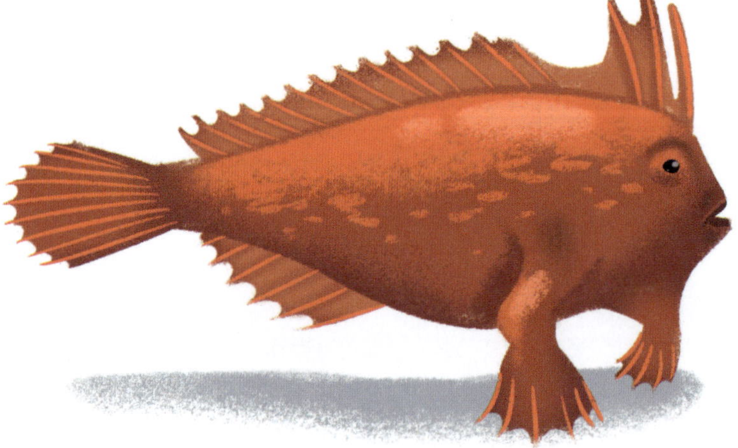